DIGITAL AND INFORMATION LITERACY ™

NEW RESEARCH TECHNIQUES
GETTING THE MOST OUT OF SEARCH ENGINE TOOLS

RYAN RANDOLPH

rosen publishing's
rosen
central®

New York

Published in 2011 by The Rosen Publishing Group, Inc.
29 East 21st Street, New York, NY 10010

Library of Congress Cataloging-in-Publication Data

Randolph, Ryan P.
New research techniques: getting the most out of search engine tools / Ryan Randolph. — 1st ed.
    p. cm. — (Digital and information literacy)
Includes bibliographical references and index.
ISBN 978-1-4488-1321-6 (lib. bdg.)
ISBN 978-1-4488-2292-8 (pbk.)
ISBN 978-1-4488-2298-0 (6-pack)
1. Internet searching—Juvenile literature. 2. Web search engines—Juvenile literature. 3. Computer network resources—Juvenile literature. I. Title.
ZA4230.R36 2010
001.4'202854678—dc22

2010016912

Manufactured in the United States of America

CPSIA Compliance Information: Batch #W11YA: For further information, contact Rosen Publishing, New York, New York, at 1-800-237-9932.

CONTENTS

INTRODUCTION

In science class, the teacher just assigned students a paper on dolphins. You also have a project on George Washington due for history class. You want to learn about the latest news story. How can you look into all of these topics? Many people today turn to the Internet.

There is a lot of information online. Web pages are created daily, and content is added to social media Web sites constantly. What is the best way to navigate it all? With all this information, it is no wonder that almost half of the people who are on the Internet use a search engine every day. Only e-mail is used more.

Most people search using one of the major search engines, such as Google. They may try an online encyclopedia, too. These steps are an acceptable start, but there are many ways to find the information you may need online. A good researcher will figure out what tools are available and which are best for the job!

Knowing how to find reliable answers to research questions using online tools is essential. Words on a Web page are not the only sources of information available. Videos, maps, and images are found on the Web, too. Additional content is posted on blogs and Web sites such as YouTube, Twitter, Wikipedia, and Flickr every day.

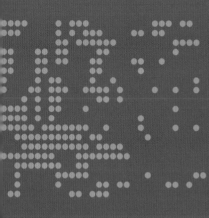

Researching answers to questions and writing papers can be done using tools and information found on the Internet. A librarian can also guide you toward helpful resources in a library's collection and databases.

There are also new ways to search across all types of content. Web sites exist that can help people learn more about a broad topic, refine searches, and find related sources. Some search engines focus on a narrow area of the Internet, such as academic resources, movies, blogs, or images. Other search engines present information in ways that go farther than a traditional Google search. In addition, there are tools that make searching and note taking easy. They move beyond creating favorites or bookmarks and include great resources for organizing research and creating a bibliography.

Having access to all these neat new tools does not mean that students can do all of their research from home. Some of the best resources for research will not appear in regular Web search results. Believe it or not, a great deal of information that is available on the Internet is not visible to Web search engines. This information is blocked from being "seen" by a search engine or requires a subscription. For example, the full text of articles in newspapers, magazines, and academic journals might not be available unless a person or institution has paid for access to the articles. A librarian can help in figuring out which databases are accessible from the library and which are best for a particular topic.

Although new research techniques and tools are great for school papers, they also have everyday uses as well. They can be used to find out the name of the actor in your favorite movie, when someone has tweeted about your favorite band, or to look at reviews of a local restaurant. New tools also make it easier than ever to share information with friends. Although Web sites and technologies come and go, a good Web searcher always has an eye on what is coming next.

Chapter 1

Some Options for Searching Online

There are many ways for researchers to find the information they are seeking online. Traditional search engines use powerful computers. Metasearch engines send a user's search terms to the major search engines and then put together the results from all the search engines. Directories rely on humans to select and maintain links organized by topic. Human-powered "ask an expert" sites rely on people to help answer questions. There are other search services that present data from across the Web in engaging ways, too.

Web Directories

In the early days of the World Wide Web, there was a small, but growing, number of Web sites. People realized there was a need to find information quickly. Web directories were an initial way to navigate the growing Web. People would review and categorize new sites on the directory. Yahoo! started out as a Web directory. Open Directory and ipl2: Information You Can Trust are other examples of Web directories. Given human categorization

There are many ways to search for information online. One method is to use a Web directory where people have selected high-quality Web sites that contain beneficial information, such as ipl2: Information You Can Trust (http://www.ipl.org).

and review, Web directories can have high-quality results but do not cover the whole Web. Web directories, as well as online encyclopedias, tend to be helpful resources when users are looking for information on specific topics, such as information about certain sites or hotels in a city. Information on current events or new advances in certain areas might be limited.

Traditional Search Engines

To deal with the explosion of information on the Web efficiently, companies have increasingly used computing power to help search the Web.

There are many search engines, but the most popular search engines today are Google, Yahoo!, Microsoft's Bing, and Ask.com. Different ranking methods are used to measure how important other people find a particular site.

The result of a search by a search engine may be thousands of links to Web pages. Usually the results on the first page or two are good to focus on. They typically contain information that can help answer a question, refine keywords used in a search, or contain links to other sources of information. These results pages may also contain links to Web sites that have paid to be placed at the top of the results page.

Searching Multiple Search Engines

A key to finding the correct answers to questions is to try different search words and tools. One way people can get information that is pulled from various search tools is by using a metasearch engine. Metasearch engines are search engines that search other search engines. Some metasearch engines include Yippy.com, Dogpile, Ixquick, InfoSpace, Surfwax, and MetaCrawler.

There are pros and cons to using a metasearch engine. There are dozens of metasearch engines at hand, but most people prefer to use a major search engine, such as Google. This is because metasearch engines may vary in the quality of their results, may take longer to run a search, and may not have the same advanced search options. Some people, though, choose metasearch engines because these can search many major search engines at once.

Other people use metasearch engines because they prefer the special features of some of these engines. For example, Ixquick maintains a user's privacy in searching by not recording a user's Internet address or search terms. Dogpile produces simple results. Yippy's search results put items into clusters that help users navigate the results. For instance, in a search for "dolphins," Yippy would show typical results, but in a sidebar on the left, it would also cluster all returns so a user could see results for the Miami

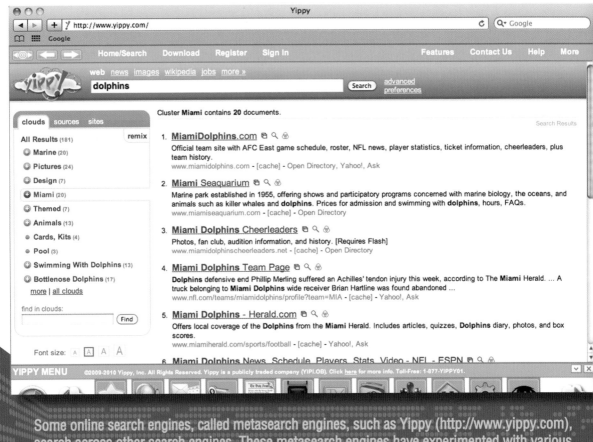

Some online search engines, called metasearch engines, such as Yippy (http://www.yippy.com), search across other search engines. These metasearch engines have experimented with various ways to present results that help refine searches.

Dolphins professional football team, a particular species of dolphin such as bottlenose, pictures of dolphins, films featuring dolphins, and more. This sidebar element can help refine or revise a search quickly.

New Search Engines, New Results

Traditional search engines provide a list of popular Web sites based on keywords that users type into the search field box of the search engine's Web page. People do not think and research like a computer. They gather information by association, they refine searches as they learn more, and then they dig deeper in certain areas.

Search engine companies recognize this practice. Consequently, search engines are getting better at helping people improve their searches. Search engines are also getting better at organizing results. They allow users to view Web pages, images, videos, blogs, and social media such as Twitter. Viewing results in varying ways helps people make connections and associations. On some newer search engines, results pages are sometimes organized more like a "desktop." They make use of tabs, drop-down menus, and sidebars. The ideal result is more knowledge data and less unusable data.

Web search engines are trying to help researchers find what they need in a more useful, efficient manner. So, when a user types in the word

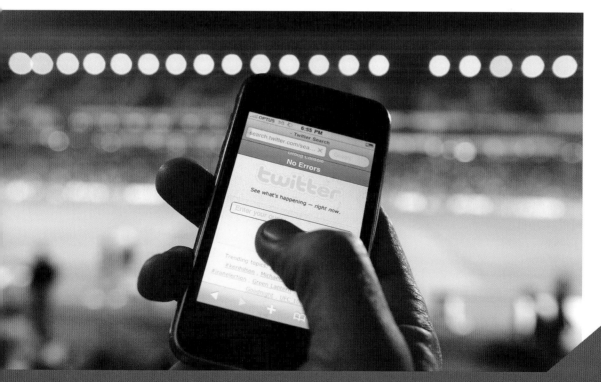

People are no longer tethered to a desk when using the Internet. Smartphones may be used to communicate with the aid of Twitter on the go, or, for example, to check favorite players' statistics while at a game.

"dolphin," the Web sites will offer results that include videos, pictures, a blog post about swimming with dolphins, or a reaction on Twitter to the Miami Dolphins' first-round draft pick. These results will be grouped in such a way as to make it easy for a user to find the set of results for which he or she is looking, whether he or she wants information on the mammal or the sports team.

Recent search engines of note include Haika, Cuil, Kosmix, Yebol, Surf Canyon, Evri, and Duck Duck Go. Most of these engines search multiple resources. They each present results differently, but typically they include sections for results from Web sites, blogs, Wikipedia, images, videos, and often Twitter. Browsys, Viewzi, Exalead, and Search Cube are other search engines that present results in new ways. Some of these allow users to organize Web sites in folders and share them with friends or present users with search results that are displayed as a three-dimensional cube.

File   Edit   View   Favorites   Tools   Help

SEMANTIC WEB SEARCH

Semantic Web Search

The newest frontiers in Web search focus on various ways to ask for information and how these results are presented. Some people use a fancy term for this idea, semantic Web search. Semantics is the study of the meaning of words. In the past, computers were not always great at returning results that captured what users were really looking for when keywords were typed into a search box. Semantic Web search simply means that search engines are getting better at interpreting the context of a search—or suggesting related search terms. Semantic Web search is a slowly developing type of searching and means different things to different people. However, it is an interesting trend in how search results are interpreted and presented, and researchers should be aware of it.

Another new direction in finding information on the Web is focused on bringing results back to a user from the Web, rather than providing only links. The "At a Glance" section of the Kosmix search results and the "zero click" box on Duck Duck Go are examples of this feature. The Web site Wolfram/Alpha has a similar focus on providing computed results rather than links.

Wolfram/Alpha calls itself a "computational knowledge engine." It looks like a search engine in that it has a search box. However, it is best used for searches that involve numbers, such as calculations, distances, times, and dates. This is a good search source if a user needs to find out

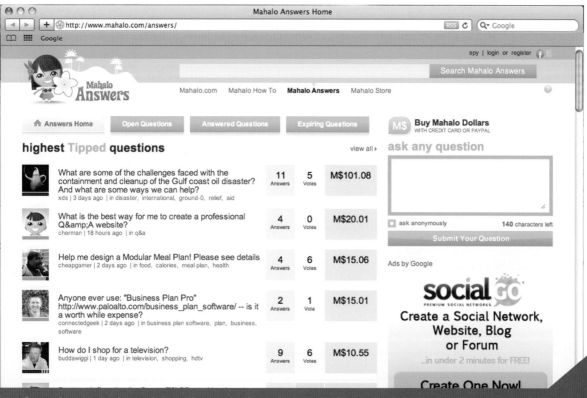

Sometimes people are better than search engines at finding answers. Some Web sites, including Mahalo (http://www.mahalo.com), allow users to ask questions on specific topics that others then try to answer.

facts about a hometown, distances between planets, statistics on a favorite sports team, or what happened on a particular date, such as the user's birthday. Google offers a service that provides some of the same benefits of Wolfram/Alpha. It is called Google Squared and can be found in the GoogleLabs section of the Web site.

Another way people find information they need, given the huge amounts of data on the Internet, is to turn to other people for help. A simple resource for students is asking a librarian for help at the local library or online. But certain Web sites specialize in allowing you to ask questions for people to answer. Answers.com, answerbag, AllExperts, Yahoo Answers, Yedda, ChaCha, and Mahalo are specific examples. These Web sites are forums where questions on given topics are asked and answered. There are answers from people related to computers, plumbing, appliances, cars, health, and more. Search engines can let you see if someone else has answered a question similar to yours on one of these forums. Unfortunately, it is hard to verify how reliable answers from these sites are. They can be suitable resources for certain questions, but they are rarely an acceptable place to research a project or paper for school.

Many of the latest search engines are worthy of note. It is challenging to determine which Web sites people will begin using. Some Web sites may no longer exist when this book is published! Even if the site disappears, many of the ideas are worthwhile and will improve how people conduct a search. The best ideas are often incorporated into the main search engines such as Google, Yahoo!, Ask, and Bing.

MYTHS&FACTS

MYTH Search engines explore the entire World Wide Web.

FACT Search engines return only public information. Information on the "invisible Web" or "deep Web" and in subscription (paid) databases usually does not turn up in an Internet search. Libraries often have purchased special databases that allow patrons to have access to the full text of newspaper, magazine, and journal articles so a patron does not have to pay for them.

MYTH A researcher needs to use only one search engine.

FACT When researching online, it is best for a researcher to try multiple search engines. Search engines differ in the Web pages that they search and how their results are presented.

MYTH Search engine results contain anything and everything related to the keywords that are entered in a search box.

FACT Not usually. It is important to refine your keyword search, use synonyms, and find unique and specialized search terms to narrow the coverage to relevant results.

→ **Chapter 2**

Search Engine Tools and Refining Results

Search results can seem overwhelming to researchers when first exploring a particular topic. There can be pages and pages of results, only some of which are helpful. So how can users quickly and efficiently refine results?

Perfecting a Search with Keywords

Searches are driven by keywords. The more specific the researcher's keyword is, the narrower or more focused the search results will be.

Using research on George Washington, the first president of the United States, as an example, if a researcher types "George Washington" in the keyword box of a search engine, does that mean "George Washington, the president," "George Washington University," or "George Washington Carver, the inventor"? When the researcher uses keywords such as "President George Washington," the results of the search will be more relevant, or to the point.

Three of the many possible results of a search for "George Washington" are shown here, clockwise from left: George Washington Carver, inventor; George Washington University; a statue of President George Washington.

As already noted, search engines are getting very effective at helping users find what they need. Many automatically offer related search terms and topics. These suggestions are not always accurate, and conducting many searches is suggested. The following are some tips for researchers to use in refining a Web search.

Improving Keywords: Related Search Terms and Synonyms

Finding unique words that are related to a topic is helpful for improving results during a search. On topics related to science, for example, this process can be fairly easy. A species name, a chemical compound, or a formula typically can provide keywords that produce more precise results.

Coming up with multiple ways to express similar concepts can also help get suitable results. Using the George Washington example again, a researcher can search for George Washington's biography, life, lifetime, history, facts, or timeline. Each related term or synonym (a word or phrase that means exactly or nearly the same as another) should provide results that give a full range of Washington's life. Sites that did not come up to the top of one search may come up to the top of another search in which the related terms or synonyms were used.

Using Phrases

Another way to focus search results is to search for a phrase using quotation marks. This feature is good for stripping away less relevant results. For example, if a person is researching a book, story, or poem for English class, using quotes around the title can be effective in limiting the results because the search engine searches for the exact phrase within the quotation marks, in the exact order the words were keyed in. The downside of phrase searching is that it may be too precise and leave out other helpful results.

Including and Excluding Keywords: Boolean Operators

Many people who teach and write about searching for information discuss the use of Boolean operators to refine users' searches. "Boolean operators" is the special phrase for the method of using the simple words "AND," "OR," and "NOT" to expand or limit a search. In some search engines, typing

There are many search engines to choose from, and search technology seems to change constantly. Some search engines such as Yahoo! and Microsoft's Bing even share search technology.

these words in capital letters in the search box will increase or decrease the search results.

Before getting too far into the function of Boolean operators, it is worth noting that Google and other search engines automatically incorporate these operators. For example, Google considers all the words in a search, so if a user includes additional keywords, Google assumes that there is an OR intended between words. Additional keywords also act as an AND function. Content that contains more of the keywords will likely be listed higher in the results. A search for "George Washington" assumes a user is looking for George OR Washington, but presents results of pages with George AND Washington first. Finally, Google uses the "-" sign instead of the word "NOT" to exclude terms. There should be no space between the "-" sign and the word a user wants to exclude. In the Washington example, this search would look like "George Washington -University" to exclude results related to George Washington University.

Search Engine Shortcuts

Web search engines have improved on how they interpret the information that users type into a search box. For example, if a person enters two numbers separated by an asterisk (*), such as "12*5," the major search engines will automatically calculate the answer, 60. If the user enters "120/2," the search engine will automatically return 60. Besides these shortcuts, an individual can also use "+" for addition and "-" with spaces between the numbers for subtraction.

Built-in Tools for Refining

People search for many subjects online. There are new technologies and ways of displaying information being created all the time. As a result, the major search engines are very good at helping users find what they are seeking. For example, major search engines now include an "autocomplete" function. When a user starts typing, the search engine suggests additional keywords. This feature helps refine searches. In addition, all the major search engines have tabs for focusing searches on only images, current news, videos, blogs, or shopping Web sites, among other options.

Often, on major search engines, after an initial search is conducted, more options appear. The location and tools available on a results page can change or shift when the search engine is redesigned. Presently on Google, for example, if a user opens the "more search tools" toolbar on the left side of the search results page, he or she can view additional tools in the Google "toolkit." If searching for current events, the user can look at only

Reverse image searching allows users to play detective on the go! A service such as Google Goggles (http://www.google.com/mobile) allows users to submit pictures of objects on their mobile devices and the search engine will search for more information on the Web using the image.

the "latest" items posted, which may include Twitter posts, or items posted over the past twenty-four hours, week, month, or year. Blogs and YouTube are also search tool options. Another method to refine results on Google is a link to find related search terms. Yet another is called the Wonder Wheel, which allows users to see related topics and how they branch off from their original keyword.

Specialized Searches

Although a major search engine is a good place to start a search, it often makes sense to go to specific Web sites, depending on the search needs. For instance, when looking for videos, pictures, or locations on a map, there may be a specific Web site from which to start the search, such as YouTube, Flickr, or MapQuest.

There are numerous map services. Google Maps and MapQuest are two useful sites for finding places, calculating distances, and seeing driving times. One of the most exciting ways to search maps is by using Google Earth. Accessing Google Earth requires downloading software that allows

If a user needs to view a specific video or news report, or locate a place on a map, one shortcut he or she can use is to go directly to a video sharing or mapping Web site.

the user to see images in 3-D and also layers in Google's local search technology. Google Earth even has maps of the moon!

Searches for pictures or images can be started on major search engines such as Yahoo! and Google. If a researcher is conducting an image search on Google, there is an interesting feature called Image Swirl. This feature will allow a researcher to look at multiple sources of an image and get ideas about how they are related to one another. A further development in image search is the Google Goggles tool, found among the Google Labs options. This tool allows users to search based on a picture. For example, a researcher could use a mobile phone to take a picture of a statue in a museum or a book in the library, and conduct a Google search based on the image. Currently, there are also numerous photo Web sites that allow users to share photos and that can be searched directly. Two major photo-sharing Web sites are Yahoo's Flickr and Google's Picasa.

If a person is looking for videos, the major search engines offer a video search. However, many user-generated videos are added directly to Web sites such as Google's YouTube, Hulu, and Vimeo, among others. Users can search these Web sites directly or via a search engine. If a user is researching orcas for a class assignment, he or she can watch informational videos about how and what orcas hunt, where they migrate, and more. Text-based sites are not the only sources for great, factual information.

There are also various ways to search for academic materials. These research techniques are important for writing papers for school assignments. An overview of the major academic resources and databases that are available to student researchers is provided in the next chapter.

TEN GREAT QUESTIONS

TO ASK A LIBRARIAN

1 What search engines do you recommend?

2 Which directories or specialized Web sites are best for learning about my topic?

3 To which databases does the library have access?

4 Where can I find primary source information?

5 Which search tools are best for video searches?

6 Where are the best sites to find pictures?

7 What sources should I use to follow current events?

8 How can I tell if the content on a Web page is reliable?

9 How do I create page-mail or text alerts?

10 Are there any browser extensions or add-ons that can help me search for my topic?

Chapter 3

Databases and Other Academic Search Tools

Search engines can return an overwhelming number of results sometimes. Search engines cannot "see" everything, though. There is much information that is available, for free, and that is visible to a search engine. People call this the "visible Web." Yet, there are also other Web sites with great information that search engines are not allowed to view or to retrieve. People call this the "invisible Web" or the "deep Web." Some of these sites include magazine, newspaper, and government Web sites.

There are a few search engines that specialize in searching the deep or invisible Web for content. They include Completeplanet, IncyWincy, DeepPeep, and DeepDyve. Although specialized search engines exist, the major search engines continue efforts to make the "invisible Web" more visible.

Still, it is often more effective for a researcher to find a database that is specialized for a topic of particular interest. One way to locate a database is to add words such as "directory" or "database" to a keyword search. This approach can lead to databases or wikis that have lists of additional

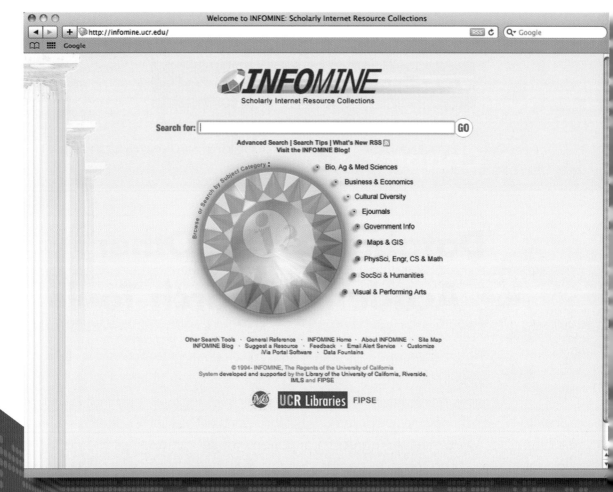

There are many scholarly search tools available to researchers, such as the librarian-maintained directory INFOMINE (http://infomine.ucr.edu). Such directories attempt to scour the "deep Web" for detailed information on academic topics.

resources related to a specific subject. An example of a directory focused on searching scholarly resources is INFOMINE. The Web site is maintained by university librarians and is designed for university students, professors, and researchers.

Google also offers resources for focused academic searches. Google Books is a reliable resource if a researcher is looking for books on a certain topic. It is a helpful first step and can be used together with a search at the local library. Searching a library's catalog for books on a computer at the library is often the best way to find what is available at that library or the network of libraries to which the library belongs. Some libraries allow a researcher to access the library's catalog from home, but others do not.

Google Scholar is another resource available to students. Google Scholar, a topic-specific search engine, focuses on searching academic literature from many fields of study. It looks across articles, theses, books,

Students and researchers sometimes can gain access to public and school libraries' catalogs from their computers at home. Some libraries even allow their patrons to download audiobooks and e-books from home.

abstracts, and court opinions. The sources of information are academic journals, universities, and other Web sites, such as JSTOR. JSTOR is a popular, free Web site that has stored academic journal articles with a wide range of subject matter. The Directory of Open Access Journals is another resource that focuses on free, full-text, journal articles. The limitation of these Web sites, though, is that they do not include articles that require a subscription.

Searching at Libraries and on Private Databases

Often a researcher might find a great journal article or newspaper story online, only to discover that it costs money to be able to read it. This is called a subscription. A customer pays a subscription amount to have access to the particular product. Publishers of newspapers, books, and journals usually charge a subscription fee because they spent money creating their products. In the case of online articles, some people do not want to pay for a whole subscription to a publication for access to only one article, though, especially if these people cannot first read it to see if the article will be helpful to their research.

Most public and many school libraries have access to various databases, often many more than those that people have available at home. The library buys the subscriptions, and library patrons get to search them for free. When doing research for a school paper or project, a researcher who visits a library can have access to important information for the assignment. There are two basic types of databases. Some databases create their own content. Others combine content and make the full text of the articles available.

Academic Databases

One type of database to which a library may subscribe combines access to magazine and newspaper articles, academic journal articles, and even

JSTOR (http://www.jstor.org) is one of several Web sites that collects and organizes academic material, mostly journal articles. JSTOR offers a high-quality archive of articles, free of charge.

videos. It is important to note that the information in the databases is often produced by a publishing company, but not the same one that produced the original articles. The databases collect content, but they are typically not producing new information. They are simply combining the information so that library users can view it.

File   Edit   View   Favorites   Tools   Help

THINKING ABOUT THE QUALITY OF REFERENCE MATERIAL FOUND ONLINE

Thinking About the Quality of Reference Material Found Online

An advantage of reference material that is available from an industry publisher is that the content has been edited, fact-checked, and typically written by an expert in the field. There are usually helpful images and illustrations related to the content, too. It is not always perfect, and it may not always be up-to-date, but it is generally of high quality and recognized by others as a valid source of information. An online encyclopedia such as Wikipedia is often a starting point for students' research. Many Wikipedia articles are of good quality and supported with sources anyone can double-check. But because anybody can edit a wiki, entries can be incorrect or contain factual errors. They can also be incomplete or lack supporting documentation. Wikipedia will often note when this circumstance is the case. The bottom line, though, is that Wikipedia should not be used as the only resource in writing an academic paper. Many people do not consider it a valid reference and will not allow its use. Sometimes it can be a good starting point for finding other Web and book sources on a topic, though.

There are a few major academic database providers. These providers include EBSCO, ProQuest, Gale (Cengage Publishing), and H. W. Wilson, among others. These companies offer a wide variety of products under different names. For example, ProQuest offers the ProQuest databases, eLibrary, and SIRS databases (originally, SIRS stood for Social Issues Resource Series). Some databases are specifically focused on topics such as history, art, science, literature, and health.

Private database search functions are often similar to the major Web search engines. A user can navigate these databases in a way that is similar to how they would navigate on a Web browser. A librarian can let users know to which databases the library has access. The librarian can also help users find the best database for their research needs.

Databases with Original Content

Another type of database to which a library may subscribe contains original content. Original content means that a publishing company has hired experts in a field to write about a particular topic. The company then makes this information available to libraries for the public to use. The result is a collection of original articles and reference materials, similar to how an encyclopedia is presented.

Two examples of companies that produce this type of database are ABC-CLIO and Facts On File. ABC-CLIO is a publisher known for its American and world history databases. Facts On File, owned by Infobase Publishing, offers original content that focuses on history, literature, and science. It also offers a news service for libraries. Other publishing companies may offer databases that focus on art, atlases, health, or science. Remember that a librarian can help users find the best database for their research!

Chapter 4

New Research Tools

Each search engine regularly introduces new tools for finding answers connected to history, current weather, restaurants, travel, and sports scores. There are related maps, images, and videos. Frequent Web searchers should stay up-to-date on the latest ways to find online information. Helpful new technologies can find their way into everyday use in places beyond Google before becoming incorporated into the major search engines. These new tools may start on a specialized search engine. They may be part of a browser, or they could get their start on what is known as a mashup between Web sites. It could be a new toolbar or an extension or add-on to a browser. Why not get a head start on these new technologies by exploring beyond the basic search tools and major search engines?

Browser Tools and Search Engine Toolbars

Many tools for efficient researching start with a browser. There are numerous Web browsers. Microsoft's Internet Explorer and Mozilla's Firefox are

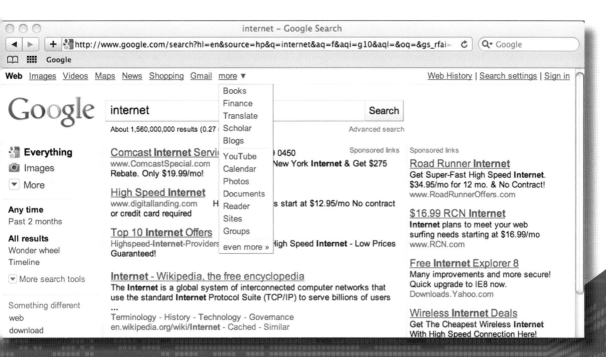

After conducting an initial search on most major search engines such as Google, users have access to a variety of tools in drop-down menus and tabs, which can be used for refining results.

the most popular, followed by Google's Chrome and Apple's Safari browsers. Browsers are great for creating bookmarks or favorites. They also allow for tabbed browsing. Tabbed browsing means instead of opening up multiple windows of a browser, a user can navigate with new tabs. This technique makes it effortless to conduct multiple searches and go back and forth between Web pages. The search engine Browsys now allows users to conduct multiple searches that mimic this tabbed browsing format all in one search engine. The major search engines such as Google and Yahoo! will allow users to focus searches on images, video, maps, or news with "tabs" at the top of results pages. All the major search engines offer toolbars that help make commonly used search tools easily accessible. They also make sharing information with others simple. These toolbars are relatively straightforward to download and are compatible with most browsers.

File   Edit   View   Favorites   Tools   Help

TOOLS FOR ORGANIZING AND CITING RESEARCH

Tools for Organizing and Citing Research

Pulling together research for a paper is like putting together a puzzle. In a puzzle, small pieces are put together to form a big picture. In a paper, pieces of research are put together to form new ideas or insights. Researchers can find those pieces of information in books and other sources online. How does a person keep track of all of those resources? Tracking sources can be challenging when a researcher jumps from link to link during the hunt for good sources of information.

Many Web sites and blogs have buttons, also called gel buttons, that enable users to print, save, download, and share information. Some Web sites also make it easy to create a citation for a research paper.

There are many tools now available to people for organizing research. One way is to use the "bookmark" or "favorite" function in a Web browser. There are new tools for managing research, however. These tools can also help the researcher create citations (sources for quotes or information) for a bibliography. Some allow people to share and recommend research and links to others.

There are many providers of software and Web sites for sharing and citing research. Examples of software that can help organize research are NoodleTools, Zotero, CiteULike, EndNote, and RefWorks. Some tools require software to be purchased, while others are Firefox browser add-ons. There are also free tools that are useful for creating citations, including EasyBib and BibMe.

Browser Add-ons

Another convenient tool for smart searching is a browser add-on or extension. A browser add-on is a piece of software that lets a person's browser do new things. There are add-ons that make searching, blogging, travel planning, Web site development, shopping, social networking, and e-mail efficient.

The Cloudlet add-on inserts a tag cloud version of results under the query box in Google. It appears before the traditional search results and is great for developing related search terms. As noted previously, Google and other search engines now also suggest related search terms.

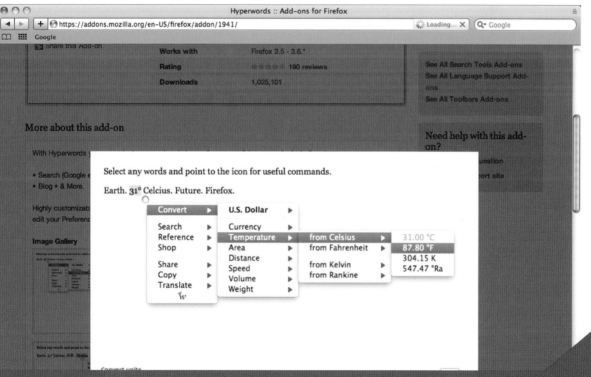

Browser add-ons make Internet surfing effortless. The Hyperwords extension for Firefox (https:// addons.mozilla.org) creates shortcuts, such as looking up a word's definition or converting a temperature from Celsius to Fahrenheit, just by highlighting a word or numeral on a Web page.

Another handy search add-on is from Surf Canyon. Surf Canyon operates its own search engine, but the add-on will modify Google search results based on links that are chosen. When the Surf Canyon extension is installed and a Google search is made for "dolphins," for example, if a person were to click a link on the bottlenose dolphin, and then go back to the Google results page, a handful of results related to the bottlenose dolphin would appear under the link that was clicked previously. The Google results refine themselves based on the links a user clicks on first!

Another example is the Hyperwords extension for Firefox, which allows a user to find additional information on any word or phrase highlighted on a text page. Right-clicking the mouse on any word will bring up menus. From these menus, a user can start another search for related Web sites, images, or videos. Users can also translate text, convert currencies, and search maps.

Staying on Top of It All

New information is available on countless topics. Many ideas being discussed every day fall outside of what traditional newspapers and cable television usually cover. Conversations people are interested in having are happening on various social media: blogs, Twitter, and Tumblr, for example. Some researchers might believe that these sorts of resources cannot help them as they investigate a subject for school. Some of the people leading these conversations may be experts on a particular topic, though. Certainly, there is a lot of information to be accessed in many different subject areas. How does someone keep up with it all? There are tools that can be used to have information sent to you automatically.

Alerts

If a person is conducting research on a topic, one way to stay on top of new information is through an e-mail or text alert. This feature is especially helpful

Researching topics online can be challenging. New tools are always being developed to help users find, organize, and share information on the Web.

if the person needs to have the latest reports on a current news story, a sports team, a particular piece of legislation, or a favorite group of musicians. Google offers an alert service that will e-mail subscribers when new results related to a user's selected keywords are available. Google alerts are free, and users can customize how often they want alerts to be sent. Many newspaper Web sites enable readers to set up alerts. There are other services that offer alerts, but they can require a subscription and may be targeted toward businesses.

RSS Feeds and Readers

A method to keep up-to-date on current news, blogs, and other Web sites that an individual likes to follow is through an RSS feed and RSS reader. RSS stands for "Really Simple Syndication." It is an elaborate way of describing a different format for a Web page. RSS feeds are used by Web sites that are frequently updated. People can view RSS feeds by using an RSS reader. With this format, people can collect new information from multiple sources. Google Reader and Bloglines are two popular RSS readers. RSS readers are helpful if a user is focused on specific Web sites or blogs that are updated at different times.

Real-Time Search and Discovery

Real-time search is the ability to find the newest information on a topic. What are journalists, experts, and regular people on the Internet saying about the latest news? Often this information is available through social media Web sites, like blog posts or Twitter.

There are specialized search engines for real-time searching. These include Collecta, Leapfish, OneRiot, Surcher, and Scoopler. Some search engines, such as Yebol, Cuil, and Kosmix, also feature a section on Twitter conversations. As with other emerging search trends, Google and others have begun to show real-time search results. These will typically appear right on the results page, and the results page will be updated with new tweets or blog posts as they are made available.

From the original sub-ject directories on the Web to real-time searching of social media, searching on the Internet is changing constantly. New tools also make it easier than ever to find information online—and to share it with friends. Some of the Web sites in this book may disappear, and new technologies and ways of surfing may replace the old ones. Staying on top of what is new and interesting can make researching a topic easy and effective.

The icon for Really Simple Syndication (RSS) feed signifies to users that a Web page is available for an RSS reader. RSS readers make it easy to check many Web sites for updates on one page, saving users time.

GLOSSARY

academic Based on school or formal learning, particularly institutions of higher education.

alerts An e-mail or text service that notifies users when new results related to selected topics are available, such as weather or news alerts.

blog A shared online journal used by people to post their insights and information about their lives, interests, and experiences.

Boolean Relating to a mathematical system of notation invented in the nineteenth century that symbolically shows relationships between things and that has been applied to the Web by using the words "AND," "NOT," and "OR" to narrow or broaden searches.

browser A software program used to access the Internet to view documents.

browser add-on A mini-program available for downloading that changes or enhances how a Web browser functions. Also known as a browser extension.

content Anything one can read, watch, or play on the Web: Web pages, games, videos, pictures, blogs, wikis, and other social media.

database An organized body of related information.

deep Web Web sites that search engines are not allowed to view, such as some magazine, newspaper, and government Web sites; also known as the invisible Web.

directory A collection of high-quality Web pages organized into subject categories by people, often librarians or subject specialists.

domain name The part of a URL (Web address) that usually specifies an organization, what type of organization it is, and where a Web page is located.

exclude To leave out or remove.

Internet A worldwide network of computer networks that all use the same protocols to exchange data.

keyword An important or descriptive word. A word that describes content (in a document, Web page, or video, for example).

link An instruction that connects one part of a program or an element on a list to another program or list.

logic A system or instance of reasoning.

metasearch engines Search services that search several individual search engines at once and then combine the results.

refine To improve or perfect.

RSS Really Simple Syndication, a format for a Web page. RSS feeds are used by Web sites that are frequently updated and read by RSS readers.

search engine A software tool that allows Web users to find information on the network.

semantic search Broadly defined, these are search services that seek to improve search results by understanding the meaning of terms being searched.

social media These are all Web sites that allow users to create and share content. These include social sites focused on networking (Facebook, MySpace), communications (blogs and microblogs), collaboration (wikis and social bookmarking), video (YouTube), music (last.fm), and gaming (the Sims, Second Life).

URL The acronym for "uniform resource locator," the address by which a Web page can be located on the Web.

Web mashup A new Web page created using data from two or more other Web pages that makes accomplishing tasks on the Internet more efficient, often by reducing the number of Web sites a person has to use.

wiki A Web site set up to allow users with access to add and edit content. "Wiki" means "fast" in Hawaiian.

FOR MORE INFORMATION

ipl2: Information You Can Trust
Drexel University
College of Information Science and Technology
3141 Chestnut Street
Philadelphia, PA 19104-2875
Web site: http://www.ipl.org
This organization is a merger of the Internet Public Library (IPL) and the Librarians'
    Internet Index (LII) Web sites. It is a volunteer-driven public service organi-
    zation that allows people to ask questions of librarians online. The Web
    site is also home to a large directory maintained by librarians. Check
    out its page for teens at http://www.ipl.org/div/teen.

Library of Congress
101 Independence Avenue SE
Washington, DC 20540-1400
(202) 707-9779
Web site: http://www.loc.gov
The Library of Congress serves as the research center for the U.S. Congress
    and is the largest library in the world. The Web site offers access to
    countless primary source documents, images, and files.

Media Awareness Network
1500 Merivale Road, 3rd floor
Ottawa, ON K2E 6Z5
Canada
(613) 224-7721
Web site: http://www.media-awareness.ca/english/index.cfm
The Web site for the Media Awareness Network contains a selection of
    digital literacy resources for students, teachers, and parents.

Pandia.com
P&S Koch
Ruselokkveien 59b
N-0251 Oslo, Norway
Web site: http://www.pandia.com
Pandia is a for-profit company that focuses on search engine marketing.
    Pandia's Web site contains helpful articles on new search technologies
    and tools. It includes a section on searching for kids and teens.
    Because the company is based in Europe, it also provides information
    on search engines and tools that are used outside the United States.

PBworks—Digital Research Tools Wiki
1825 South Grant Street, Suite 850
San Mateo, CA 94402
(866) 945-4463
Web site: http://digitalresearchtools.pbworks.com
PBworks is a company that hosts wikis and other collaboration tools for
    business and education. It has created a wiki maintained by volunteers
    that focuses on digital research tools.

Web Sites

Due to the changing nature of Internet links, Rosen Publishing has developed
an online list of Web sites related to the subject of this book. This site is
updated regularly. Please use this link to access this list:

http://www.rosenlinks.com/dil/nrt

FOR FURTHER READING

Gaines, Ann Graham. *Ace Your Internet Research* (Ace It! Information Literacy). Berkeley Heights, NJ: Enslow Publishers, 2009.

Hawthorne, Kate, and Daniela Sheppard. *The Young Person's Guide to the Internet*. 2nd ed. New York, NY: Routledge, 2005.

Haycock, Ken, Barbara Edwards, and Michelle Dober. *The Neal-Schuman Authoritative Guide to Kids' Search Engines, Subject Directories, and Portals*. New York, NY: Neal-Schuman Publishers, 2003.

Hock, Randolph. *The Extreme Searcher's Internet Handbook*. 2nd ed. Medford, NJ: CyberAge Books, 2007.

Porterfield, Jason. *Conducting Basic and Advanced Searches* (Digital and Information Literacy). New York, NY: Rosen Publishing, 2010.

Turabian, Kate L. Revised by Wayne C. Booth, Gregory G. Colomb, and University of Chicago Press Staff. *A Manual for Writers of Research Papers, Theses, and Dissertations: Chicago Style for Students and Researchers*. 7th ed. Chicago, IL: University of Chicago Press, 2007.

Witten, Ian, Marco Gori, and Teresa Numerico. *Web Dragons: Inside the Myths of Search Engine Technology*. San Francisco, CA: Morgan Kaufmann, 2006.

Barker, Joe, and Saifon Obromsook. "Evaluating Web Pages: Techniques to Apply & Questions to Ask." Teaching Library Workshops. University of California, Berkeley Library. August 11, 2009. Retrieved March 20, 2010 (http://www.lib.berkeley.edu/TeachingLib/Guides/Internet/Evaluate.html).

Byrne, Richard. "Beyond Google." October 24, 2009. Retrieved March 20, 2010 (http://www.freetech4teachers.com/2009/10/beyond-google-improve-your-search.html).

Casella, Dena. "Google Rolls Out Real-Time Search and Google Goggles App." *Digital Trends*, December 7, 2009. Retrieved March 22, 2010 (http://www.digitaltrends.com/mobile/google-rolls-out-real-time-search-options-and-google-goggles-app).

Dochartiagh, Niall O. *Internet Research Skills*. Thousand Oaks, CA: Sage Publications Inc., 2007.

Harris, Robert. "Internet Search Tips and Strategies." VirtualSalt.com, July 6, 2000. Retrieved March 27, 2010 (http://virtualsalt.com/howlook.htm).

Mashable.com "Five Things Wolfram Alpha Does Better (And Vastly Different) Than Google." May 19, 2009. Retrieved March 16, 2010 (http://mashable.com/2009/05/19/wolfram-alpha-better-than-google).

Purdy, Kevin. "Top 10 Must-Have Firefox Extensions, 2009 Edition." Lifehacker.com, April 11, 2009. Retrieved March 22, 2010 (http://lifehacker.com/5205629/top-10-must+have-firefox-extensions-2009-edition).

Radford, Marie L., Susan Barnes, and Linda Barr. *Web Research: Selecting, Evaluating, and Citing*. 2nd ed. Boston, MA: Allyn and Bacon, 2005.

Shaw, Maura. *Mastering Online Research: A Comprehensive Guide to Effective and Efficient Search Strategies*. Cincinnati, OH: Writers Digest Books, 2007.

INDEX

About the Author

Ryan Randolph, a writer who lives in Massachusetts, has kept current on new research techniques in the course of his education, career, and writing interests. He also researches trends in finance using search engines, blogs, alerts, RSS feeds, and wikis.

Photo Credits

Cover, pp. 1 (far left), 17 (left) Archive Photos/Getty Images; cover, pp. 1 (left), 5 Jupiterimages/Brand X Pictures/Thinkstock; cover, pp. 1 (right), 21 Bloomberg via Getty Images; cover, pp. 1 (far right), 17 (bottom right), 22 Saul Loeb/AFP/Getty Images; p. 8 Reproduced with permission from copyright 2010 by the ipl2 Consortium (http://www.ipl.org). All rights reserved; p. 11 Cameron Spencer/Getty Images; p. 17 (top right) The Washington Post/Getty Images; p. 19 Justin Sullivan/Getty Images; p. 26 © 1994–2010 INFOMINE, The Regents of the University of California System developed and supported by the Library of the University of California, Riverside, IMLS, and FIPSE; p. 27 Digital Vision/Thinkstock; p. 29 Permission provided courtesy of ITHAKA. © 2010 ITHAKA. All rights reserved; pp. 34, 37, 39 Shutterstock.com.

Designer: Nicole Russo; Editor: Kathy Kuhtz Campbell;
Photo Researcher: Karen Huang